PIANO / VOCAL / GUITAR

ABOMINABLE

MUSIC FROM THE MOTION PICTURE SOUNDTRACK

ISBN 978-1-5400-8093-6

Visit Hal Leonard Online at
www.halleonard.com

Contact us:
Hal Leonard
7777 West Bluemound Road
Milwaukee, WI 53213
Email: info@halleonard.com

In Europe, contact:
Hal Leonard Europe Limited
42 Wigmore Street
Marylebone, London, W1U 2RN
Email: info@halleonardeurope.com

In Australia, contact:
Hal Leonard Australia Pty. Ltd.
4 Lentara Court
Cheltenham, Victoria, 3192 Australia
Email: info@halleonard.com.au

CONTENTS

BEAUTIFUL LIFE

Words and Music by BEBE REXHA,
SAMUEL JAMES ZAMMARELLI, CHRISTOPHER TEMPEST,
NICK BLACK and DAVID SAINT FLEUR

*Lead vocal written an octave higher.

9

FIX YOU

Words and Music by GUY BERRYMAN,
JON BUCKLAND, WILL CHAMPION
and CHRIS MARTIN

DREAMS

Words and Music by PHILIP BERNARD BEAUDREAU
and ANDREW TYSON BISSELL

can feel like a bat - tle, when the light ___ of a vic-

- to - ry ___ seems ___ low. But we ___

___ will o - ver - come ___ the storms and the shad -

- ows, 'cause each ___ of us ___ are strong - er than ___ we know. ___

GIRL'S GOTTA

Words and Music by ANDREW TYSON BISSELL
and AMY FRANCES STROUP

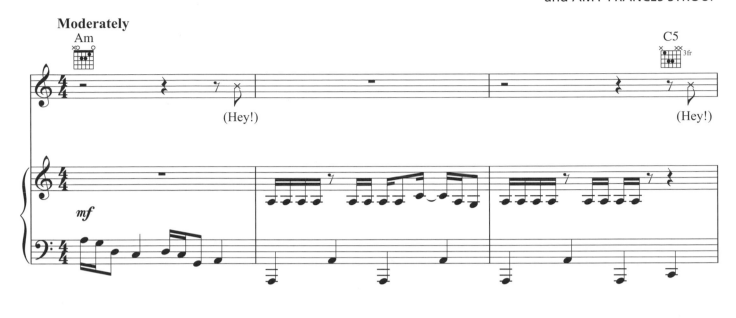

girl's got-ta do what a girl's got-ta do, what a girl's got-ta do, what a,...
(Hey!) (Hey!) (Hey!) (Hey!)

A5 C6 D5

Am
(Hey!) A girl's got-ta do what a girl's got-ta do. (Hey!) A

girl's got-ta do what a girl's got-ta do. I ain't stay-ing in the

YI AND EVEREST DUET

Words and Music by
RUPERT GREGSON-WILLIAMS

Moderately slow

Pedal ad lib. throughout

STARRY NIGHT BECOMES
A WIPE OUT

Words and Music by
RUPERT GREGSON-WILLIAMS

Moderately, expressively

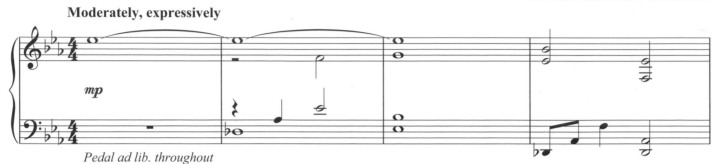

mp

Pedal ad lib. throughout

Slightly faster

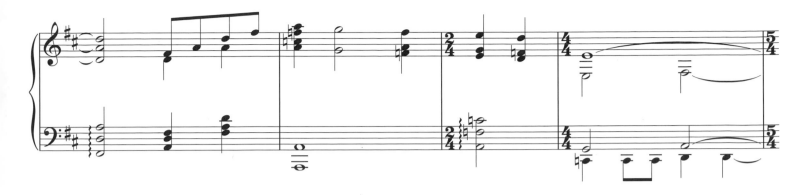

Moderately, steadily

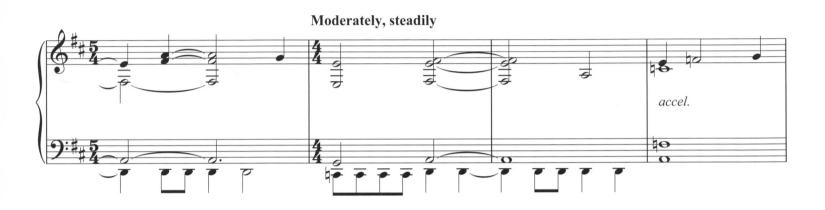

Faster

FINALLY HOME
(EVEREST)

Words and Music by
RUPERT GREGSON-WILLIAMS

Moderately slow

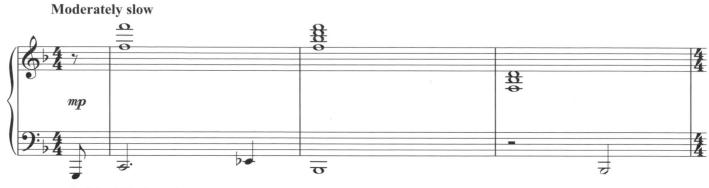

Pedal ad lib. throughout

LESHAN BUDDHA

Words and Music by
RUPERT GREGSON-WILLIAMS

Moderately

Pedal ad lib. throughout